SWITCH ON, SWITCH OFF

By Melvin Berger   Illustrated by Carolyn Croll

Thomas Y. Crowell   New York

Other Recent Let's-Read-and-Find-Out Science Books® You Will Enjoy

Ducks Don't Get Wet • Feel the Wind • The Skeleton Inside You • Digging Up Dinosaurs • Tornado Alert • The Sun: Our Nearest Star • The Beginning of the Earth • Eclipse • Dinosaur Bones • Glaciers • Snakes Are Hunters • Danger—Icebergs! • Comets • Evolution • Rockets and Satellites • The Planets in Our Solar System • The Moon Seems to Change • Ant Cities • Get Ready for Robots! • Gravity Is a Mystery • Snow Is Falling • Journey into a Black Hole • What Makes Day and Night • Air Is All Around You • Turtle Talk • What the Moon Is Like • Hurricane Watch • Sunshine Makes the Seasons • My Visit to the Dinosaurs • The BASIC Book • Bits and Bytes • Germs Make Me Sick! • Flash, Crash, Rumble, and Roll • Volcanoes • Dinosaurs Are Different • What Happens to a Hamburger • Meet the Computer • How to Talk to Your Computer • Rock Collecting • Is There Life in Outer Space? • All Kinds of Feet • Flying Giants of Long Ago • Rain and Hail • Why I Cough, Sneeze, Shiver, Hiccup & Yawn • You Can't Make a Move Without Your Muscles • The Sky Is Full of Stars • No Measles, No Mumps for Me

The *Let's-Read-and-Find-Out Science Book* series was originated by Dr. Franklyn M. Branley, Astronomer Emeritus and former Chairman of the American Museum-Hayden Planetarium, and was formerly co-edited by him and Dr. Roma Gans, Professor Emeritus of Childhood Education, Teachers College, Columbia University. For a complete catalog of Let's-Read-and-Find-Out Science Books, write to Thomas Y. Crowell Junior Books, Harper & Row, Publishers, Inc., 10 East 53rd Street, New York, NY 10022.

Let's-Read-and-Find-Out Science Book is a registered trademark of Harper & Row, Publishers, Inc.

Library of Congress Cataloging-in-Publication Data
Berger, Melvin.
  Switch on, switch off / by Melvin Berger ; illustrated by Carolyn Croll.
    p.   cm. — (Let's-read-and-find-out science book)
  Summary: Explains how electricity is produced and transmitted, how to create electricity using wire and a magnet, how generators supply electricity for cities, and how electricity works in homes.
  ISBN 0-690-04784-3 : $
  ISBN 0-690-04786-X (lib. bdg.) : $
  1. Electricity—Juvenile literature. [1. Electricity.] I. Croll, Carolyn, ill. II. Title. III. Series.
QC527.2.B47 1989
537—dc19

88-17638
CIP
AC

SWITCH ON, SWITCH OFF

It's time to go to sleep. You go to your bedroom. The room is dark. You flip up the switch on the wall. The light goes on.

You get into your pajamas. Just before you jump into
bed, you flip down the switch. The light goes off.

Flip up—the light goes on. Flip down—the light goes off. It seems like magic. But it's not magic at all. It's electricity!

Electricity is a form of energy. Energy is anything that does work.

You have lots of energy. Your energy lets you walk, run, throw a ball, ride a bike—and sometimes even clean your room!

Electrical energy also does work. It lights your house. It brings you sound from your radio. If you have an electric stove, it cooks your food. If you have an air conditioner, it keeps you cool.

Your energy comes from the food you eat. But electrical energy has to be made.

You can make electricity by yourself. You'll need a piece of electrical wire about two yards long. Ask an adult to help strip the insulation off the ends of the wire.

You'll also need a bar magnet and a compass. The compass will show whether or not you are making electricity.

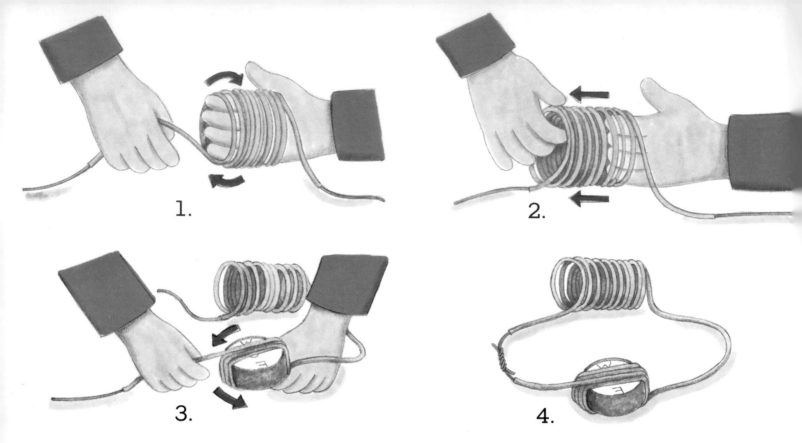

1. Wrap one end of the wire around your hand about ten times, to make a coil. 2. Slide the coil off your hand. 3. Now wrap the other end of the wire around the compass about five times. Leave the wire there. 4. Then twist the two metal ends of the wire together to make one big loop.

5. Slide the magnet quickly back and forth inside the coil. This makes electricity flow in the wire. Look at the compass as you do this. Do you see the needle move? The moving needle tells you that electricity is flowing.

But how does electricity flow through a wire?

The wire is made up of billions of tiny bits, or particles. They are called atoms. Each atom is much too small to be seen. But each atom has even smaller particles. Some of these move in paths around the atom's center. They are the electrons.

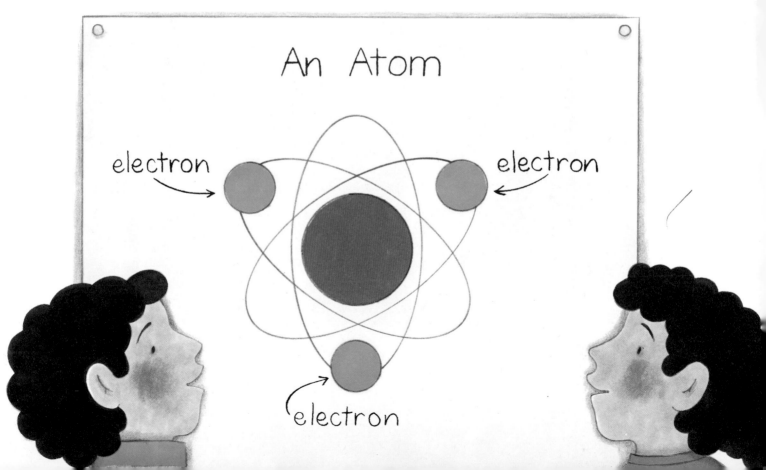

An Atom

electron

electron

electron

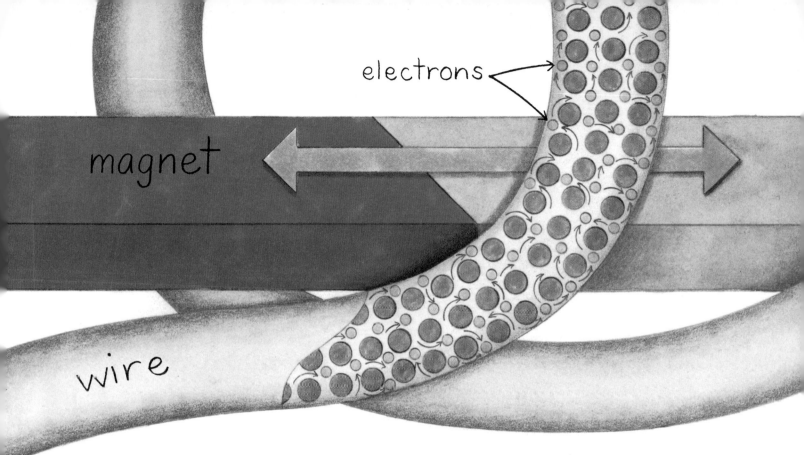

electrons

magnet

wire

Moving the magnet near the wire makes the electrons move out of their paths. They speed from atom to atom. The speeding electrons are what we call electricity.

The opposite works, too. Moving a coil of wire near a magnet also makes electricity flow.

15

Any machine that makes electricity is called a generator. Your little generator made a tiny bit of electricity. But it takes very big generators to supply electricity for a whole city.

These generators have huge coils and giant magnets.
Most generators spin a magnet inside the coils. Others
spin coils between two magnets.

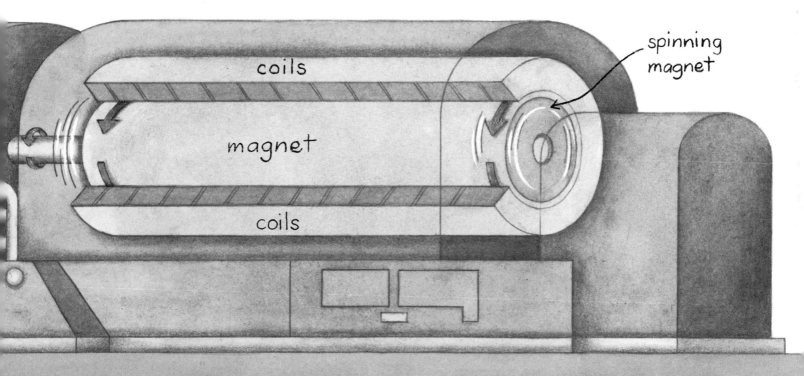

coils

spinning
magnet

magnet

coils

The muscles in your arms supplied the power for your little generator. But big generators need much more power to spin their coils or magnets. This power can come from—

wind...

flowing water...

steam....

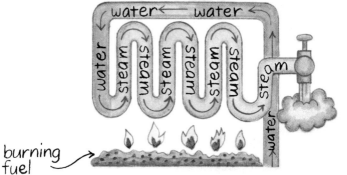

water ← water ←

water steam steam steam steam steam steam steam

water

burning fuel →

As the coils or magnets spin, electricity flows in the coils. The big wire coils are connected to other wires.

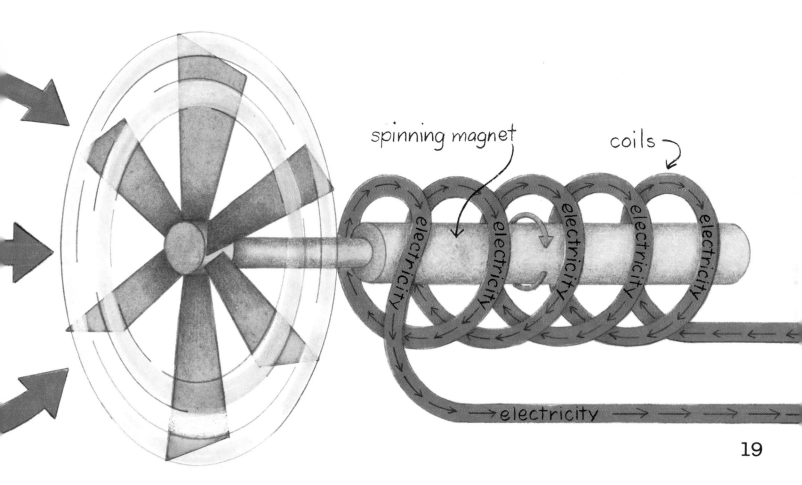

spinning magnet

coils

electricity

electricity

electricity

electricity

electricity

electricity

These wires are strung along the tops of tall poles. The electricity travels through the wires for many miles.

Shorter wires branch off from the long wires. They bring electricity to the homes, schools, stores, and other places that need it. One of these wires goes to your house.

If you live in the country or in a small town, you can
probably see the wire that brings the electricity into
your house. If you live in a big city, you may not see the
wire because it is under the ground.

Each wire is really made up of two separate wires.
One brings the electricity from the generator into your
house. The other takes the electricity back to the
generator.

Electricity flows to
the generator.

Electricity flows to
your house.

A CIRCUIT

generator

electricity

When you made your little generator, you tied the ends of the wire together. That made a loop, or circuit. Electricity always travels in a circuit. It only flows if it can get back to its starting point. If there is a break in the circuit, the electricity does not flow at all.

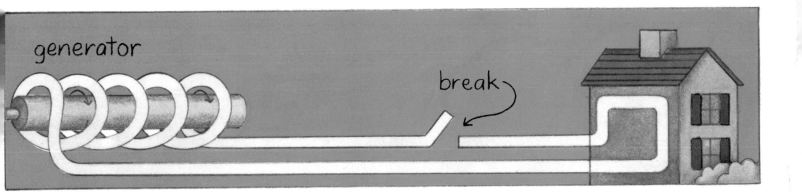

generator

break

The circuit that comes into your house splits into many other circuits. It is like many small roads coming off a big highway. All the circuits in your house have breaks in them. The breaks let you turn the electricity on and off. That's what the switch is for!

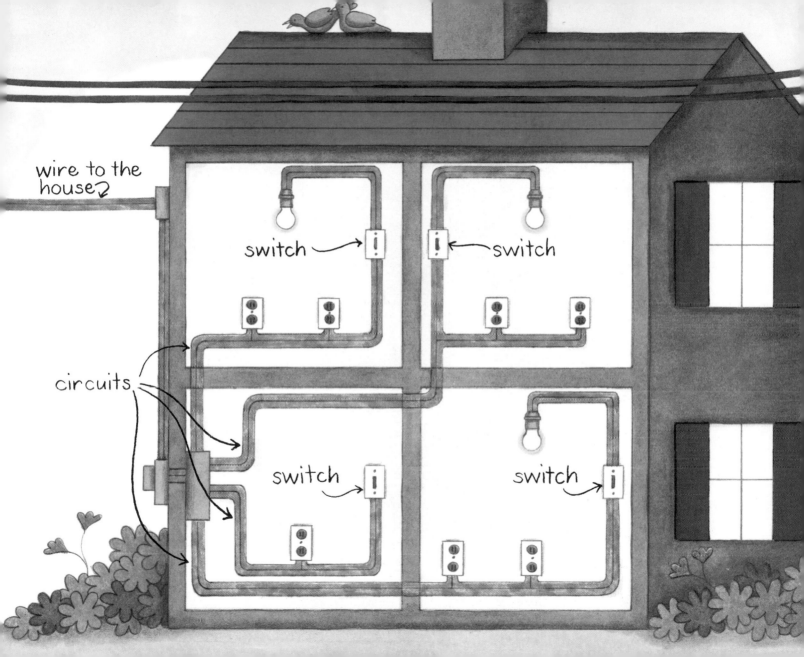

wire to the house↲

switch →

← switch

circuits

switch →

switch →

The in and out wires of one circuit meet at the light switch in your room. When the switch is down, the break in the wire is open. No electricity can flow. The light is off.

Flip up the switch. The break is closed. Now the electricity can travel through the wire to the bulb on the ceiling. The light goes on.

light off

switch down

break open

light on

switch up

break closed

Inside the bulb, there is a very thin wire. The electricity must squeeze through this wire. When it does, the wire heats up. The wire quickly becomes white-hot. The glow of the white-hot wire in the bulb lights your bedroom.

From the bulb, the electricity zips back to the switch. And from there it returns to the generator.

thin wire

Maybe you have a lamp instead of a ceiling light. The lamp has a plug at the end of its wire. The plug has two metal prongs. Electricity can flow through the prongs just as it does through wires.

You fit the plug into an electrical outlet in the wall.

The two wires of the house circuit are connected to the two holes of the outlet. When you put the plug in the outlet, the electricity can flow through the outlet, the plug, and the wire, and into the lamp.

The lamp has a switch. When you turn the lamp switch on, the electricity flows through the bulb and back out through the house circuit.

The next time you get ready for bed, stop and think.
"Switch on" means you closed the circuit. The electricity
flows.

"Switch off" means you broke the circuit. The electricity cannot flow.

Then it is dark and time to sleep. Good night.
Pleasant dreams.